IRISH TRIVIA

IRISH TRIVIA

Mary A. McCaffery

Henry M. Quinlan

Michael P. Quinlin

WINGS BOOKS
NEW YORK • AVENEL, NEW JERSEY

This 1990 edition is published by Wings Books,
distributed by Outlet Book Company, Inc.
a Random House Company,
40 Engelhard Avenue,
Avenel, New Jersey 07001,
by arrangement with Quinlan Press.
Original edition published
by Quinlan Press, Inc. in 1985.

Manufactured in the United States of America

Library of Congress Cataloging-in-Publication Data
McCaffery, Mary A.
    Irish trivia / by Mary A. McCaffery, Henry M. Quinlan,
  Michael P. Quinlin.
        p.   cm.
    Reprint. Originally published: Boston, MA: Quinlan Press, © 1985.
    ISBN 0-517-69909-5
    1. Ireland—Miscellanea.   2. Irish Americans—Miscellanea.
  3. Questions and Answers.   I. Quinlan, Henry M.   II. Quinlin,
  Michael P.   III. Title.
  DA906.M33   1990
  941.5'0076—dc20   89-18282
  CIP

9 8 7 6 5

Says Herself to Myself:
"We're as good as the best of them."
                    Patrick Joseph McCall

Contents

IRISH TRIVIA

QUESTIONS

GENERAL

1. "We are willing to fight for" is the first line of what pledge?

2. What is the significance of St. Patrick's blue?

3. What is the oldest heraldic symbol of Ireland?

4. Whose harp is preserved at Trinity College?

5. A traditional Irish greeting is *"Dia's Muire dhuit."* What does it mean?

6. Who are known as "the innocents" in Ireland?

7. What town in Ireland received the survivors of the *Lusitania*?

8. When would a tourist in Ireland be on time for the West Kerry Rain Festival?

9. What is a *curragh*?

10. What is known as the "Four-Faced Liar"?

11. What does the word "Cork" refer to?

12. What do Frank O'Connor, Sean O'Faolain and David Corkery have in common?

13. Who was the first Republican mayor of Cork?

14. After Thomas MacCurtain was murdered, who succeeded him as mayor of Cork?

15. What do the bogs consist of?

16. Where are most of the turf bogs?

17. Who are the "White Moths"?

18. What is the name of homemade whiskey?

19. Who gather at the Puck Fair in Killorglin?

20. Who replaced the Druids when Ireland became Christianized?

21. What are the dimensions of a hurling field?

22. What is the oldest of the great Irish illuminated manuscripts?

23. How long are the periods in Gaelic football?

24. What is *camogie*?

25. Where is Joyce Country?

26. What was the shillelagh originally used for?

27. What is Ireland's "national walking stick"?

28. Who was St. Malachy?

29. What is "keening"?

30. What is given to nursing mothers in Dublin hospitals?

31. What options did Cromwell give to defeated Irish landowners?

32. Who is nicknamed "The Cruiser" in Ireland?

33. Who is called "Mary of the Gaels"?

34. Who is responsible for an international airport being built in Knock, Co. Mayo?

35. What is the longest geographical name in Ireland?

36. What is the first day of the Celtic new year?

37. What does *gan tir gan teanga* mean?

38. What is the New Ireland Forum?

39. Where is Ireland's first Moslem mosque being built?

40. Who was President of the International Olympic Committee from 1972 to 1980?

41. What percentage of Australians are of Irish extraction?

42. Where is the annual matchmaking festival held in Ireland?

43. What Irishman won the Nobel Prize for Physics?

44. How many Argentinians are there of Irish ancestry?

45. Name the famous race horse kidnapped in 1983 but never recovered?

46. Where is the home of the famous Claddagh ring?

47. Name the Irish priest jailed in the Phillipines on unfounded murder charges.

48. Who is Andy Tyrie?

49. Who was Lawrence of Arabia?

50. What are the seven distinctly Irish breeds of dog?

51. What is the most common surname in Ireland?

52. What Irish scientist discovered the optical-mechanical analogy?

53. What weed is often called "the Irish daisy"?

54. What are the areas in Ireland where "Irish" is spoken as the first language?

55. How many men are there on a Gaelic football team?

56. Name the Irishman who won the silver medal in the 1984 Olympic marathon.

57. What is a pampootie?

58. Who is the Glendalough Saint?

59. Who was called the "Nun of Kenmare"?

60. Who founded Fianna Fáil?

61. Who was Edmund Ignatius Rice?

62. What happened to Sir Roger Casement?

63. Who was "The Irish Giant"?

64. What city is "Ireland's Canterbury"?

65. In what part of Dublin is St. Patrick's Cathedral located?

66. What is the name of the company that operates the boats between Dun Laoghaire and England?

67. In what month is the Cork International Opera Festival held?

68. What is a "Good Room"?

69. "The Creature" and "The Jar" are other terms for what substance?

70. In what month is the Dublin Horse show held in Ballsbridge?

71. What are the "poor man's version of B'nai B'rith brickbats"?

72. Approximately how many Americans are of Irish descent?

73. A farmhand from Carrick-on-Suir, he rose to international fame by winning the Super Prestige Pernod Trophy. Who is he?

74. Who stole the Blarney stone slab from the 1951 San Francisco exhibit?

75. The first major league All Star Game played in 1933 was an Irish managers' battle. Who were they?

76. Who was the copper king of Montana?

77. Who were the two Irish American baseball players — "the grand old men of baseball" — who helped organize the American League?

78. Who was the "barefooted Babe Ruth" of Irish hurling?

79. What was the significance of the Women's Marathon in Dublin in 1983?

80. What is Mothering Sunday?

81. Who was "Hannibal Hotpot"?

82. Where in Ireland did an oil tanker explode in 1979, killing 60 people?

83. Who described the Aran Islands as "a wilderness of stone and stone walls"?

84. Is Ireland a member of NATO?

85. What is Ireland's greatest energy source?

86. Who said, "I have hated God's enemies with a perfect hate"?

87. What river runs through Derry City?

88. Who are the fairy women who foretell death?

89. What is a *púca*?

90. What modern celebration had its origins in the Druid Festival of Samhain?

91. What is the traditional craft of the Tinkers?

92. Who are the "Straw Boys"?

93. Where are Ireland's world famous show ponies raised?

94. What is road bowling?

95. What are the "drags"?

96. How many bridges cross the Liffey?

97. What is peat primarily used for?

98. "Black Pool" is another name for which Irish City?

99. What is Dublin Castle used for today?

100. What colors are used on all Irish light-houses?

101. What is the "capital" of the Midlands?

102. What is a "VAT"?

103. On what day would you see the Wren Boys?

104. Where, in Ireland, was the film *Ryan's Daughter* filmed?

105. In what country are Irish troops presently stationed as a UN peace-keeping force?

106. "The Irish people are by right a free people" is from what document?

107. Who did the Irish Free State choose to design Irish coinage in 1921?

108. What is one shilling equivalent to in today's Irish money?

109. Who is the patron saint of Ireland?

110. The Irish flag has three colors: green, white and orange. Which color is on the left side of the flag?

111. Who bought Durnish Island off the Mayo Coast in 1967 and called it "the most peaceful place on Earth"?

112. What office does the Taoiseach hold?

113. When was the tri-color flag adopted as the official flag of Ireland?

114. What is the Dáil Eireann?

115. Who is the female patron saint of Ireland?

116. Irish sweaters are made from an unscoured, unbleached wool. What is it called?

117. What does the hands on a Claddagh ring symbolize?

118. What does the heart on a Claddagh ring symbolize?

119. What does the crown on a Claddagh ring symbolize?

120. What castle did Ronald Reagan stay in when he visited Ireland?

121. Where did pilots Alcock and Brown land after the first non-stop trans-Atlantic airplane flight in 1919?

122. What is a *Seanchai*?

123. Who said "The Irish are a fair people—they never speak well of one another"?

124. What is the highest salary paid to an athlete who plays under the Gaelic Athletic Association?

125. Whose picture is on the Irish 20-pound note?

126. On the last Sunday in July, many Catholics, following a long tradition, do penance by climbing what mountain?

127. What is the ancient Irish alphabet called?

128. Who is the mother of all fighting Irishwomen?

GEOGRAPHY

1. Where are St. Stephen's Green and Merrian and Fitzwilliam Squares in relation to the River Liffey?

2. How many square miles is Ireland?

3. How many miles of shoreline does Ireland have?

4. How many miles are there from Ireland to America?

5. How long is the Shannon River?

6. What is the highest mountain in Ireland?

7. What is the largest lake in Ireland?

8. What is the population of Ireland?

9. What county are the Aran Islands in?

10. How many counties are there in the Republic of Ireland?

11. What are the six counties in Northern Ireland?

12. What is the main harbor for Dublin?

13. What county is known as the Garden of Ireland?

14. What saint lived in Glendalough?

15. What does Glendalough mean?

16. At what county does the Celtic Sea and the Atlantic Ocean meet?

17. On what river is Ennistymon?

18. In what county are the Cliffs of Moher?

19. What are the four provinces of Ireland?

20. What is the name of the main shopping street in Dublin?

21. In what direction does the River Liffey flow?

22. What four bodies of water surround Ireland?

23. How large is St. Stephen's Green?

24. In what area of Dublin is the Dublin Horse Show held?

25. Where did John F. Kennedy's grandfather come from?

26. What is the name of the islands off the coast of Wexford?

27. What is the smallest county in Ireland?

28. Where does the Irish Derby take place?

29. Where is the College of St. Patrick?

30. Where was the *Book of Kells* produced?

31. What is known as the "Rebel City"?

32. Where is the grave of W.B. Yeats?

33. Where is the Fanad Peninsula?

34. Which Irish bridge is as wide as it is long?

35. In 1152, Ireland was divided into four ecclesiastical provinces. Name them.

36. What percentage of the land in Ireland is used for agriculture?

37. How many miles separate Ireland and Great Britain at their closest point?

38. What is the distance between Dublin and Cork?

39. Where are the Mourne Mountains?

40. Where did French Troops land in 1798 to help in the Rebellion?

41. Where are Ireland's three most famous caves?

42. What is the largest inland county in Ireland?

43. How many species of fish are found off of Ireland's coastline?

44. Where was Handel's Messiah first performed?

45. In which county is the famous Ardmore Round Tower?

46. What is Cork's twin city in America?

47. Where is Grosse Island, and what significance did it have to Irish emigrants in the 19th century?

48. What is Ireland's largest island?

49. Where was John Barry, "Father of the U.S. Navy," born?

50. Where are the All-Ireland Hurling Finals traditionally played?

51. Where is the Puck Fair held each year?

52. Where was Irish tenor John McCormack born?

53. Where was the Virgin Mary reputed to have appeared at the turn of the century?

54. What is Ballyporeen, Tipperary, famous for?

55. Where was Eamon DeValava born?

56. In what county is an international airport now being built?

57. Where is the principle Catholic seminary in Ireland?

58. Name the three Aran Islands.

59. What is the Saltee Island off Wexford famous for?

60. What is the City of Seven Hills, and for what is it renowned?

61. Where was Christopher Columbus' last port-of-call before discovering America?

62. Ireland is the leading European producer of what mineral?

63. What is the longest river in Ireland?

64. Where is the Giant's Causeway and how was it formed?

65. Name the nine counties of Ulster.

66. Where is the world's first interferon plant located?

67. Where is the oldest prehistoric burial tomb located in Ireland?

68. What city recently celebrated its 500th anniversary?

69. According to legend, what Irishman sailed to America in 550 A.D.?

70. Where is 'Atlantic Drive'?

71. What island is called the Emerald Isle of the Caribbean?

72. Where is Dublin Airport?

73. On what hill is Dublin Castle located?

74. On what street is the American Embassy?

75. What is the most northerly county in Ireland?

76. What is the biggest port in Ireland?

77. Where is the Abbey Theater located?

78. On what side of the Liffey is the Guinness Brewing Company located?

79. What was the name of the castle where Maynooth now stands?

80. Where is the Dunbay Castle located?

81. In what county is the Rock of Cashel?

82. What province is Cork in?

83. What are the chief rivers of Cork?

84. Where is the Burren located?

85. What other name is Sligo County known as?

86. Where is the Blarney Stone?

87. Where is Sally Gap?

88. How many miles are there between Dublin and Limerick?

89. Where is a celtic cross in Belgium?

90. What is the height of the Cliffs of Moher?

91. What city is at the head of Ardbear Bay?

92. What state in the United States is the approximate size of Ireland?

93. Where is the Martello Tower made famous by James Joyce?

94. Where is St. Patrick's Purgatory?

95. Where is St. Lawrence's Gateway?

96. What is the name of the river that runs below Lismore Castle in County Waterford?

97. Where is the Moydrum Castle?

98. What is referred to as "The Naples of Ireland"?

99. What side of the Liffey is the Custom House on ?

100. Where are famous fishermen sweaters made in Ireland?

101. Where did President Reagan stay in Co. Mayo in 1984?

102. One of the world's greatest bird sanctuaries is off the coast of Kerry. What is its name?

103. Where is the "Harbor of Tears"?

104. Where is Druid Hill?

105. Which city in Ireland could be called Erin's Venice?

HISTORY

1. What was the Northern Ireland Civil Rights Association?

2. When was Belfast first blitzed by the Germans?

3. Who was the leader of the Irish Parliamentary Party which promoted Home Rule through legislation?

4. Who read the Proclamation of the Republic on the steps of the Post Office in 1916?

5. When did St. Patrick first arrive in Ireland?

6. When was Ireland admitted to the United Nations?

7. Who was Ireland's ally in the Battle of Kinsale in 1601?

8. When was St. Oliver Plunkett executed?

9. Who was the first Catholic elected to British Parliament?

10. Who countermanded the orders to proceed with the Easter Rising? A "counter-countermanding order" followed.

11. When did RTE first broadcast?

12. Who was the founding father of the Argentinian Navy?

13. Ireland was formally proclaimed a republic on what date?

14. Who said, "I decided some time ago that if Gladstone went for Home Rule, the Orange card was the one to play"?

15. Who was hanged at Mountjoy Prison on November 1, 1920?

16. Who was the Ulsterman who led the fight against Home Rule in 1916?

17. What is the emblem of the Fenians?

18. Who were the Whiteboys?

19. Name the mayor of Cork who died on a hunger strike.

20. Who was the first Northern Irish woman elected to the British Parliament?

21. Where and when was Michael Collins killed?

22. Who was called the "Uncrowned King of Ireland"?

23. What was the Rock of Cashel famous for since the 4th century?

24. Who was known as "Orange Peel"?

25. During what era did the Irish add the prefixes "Mac" (son of) and "O" (grandson of) to their last name?

26. What is the "Lia Fail"?

27. Who wrote *The Fall Of Feudalism in Ireland*?

28. What was "Laudabiter"?

29. What brought the Sunningdale Agreement down in 1974?

30. Who had the leaders of the Easter 1916 uprising executed?

31. What replaced the Land League?

32. What was the New Departure?

33. In the early 1600's, over 100,000 orphaned Irish children were shipped as slaves to an English colony. Name the colony.

34. When was the Orange Order founded?

35. Who donated £5 to the Irish people and £100 to a dog kennel during the height of the famine?

36. What was the Kilmainham Treaty of 1882?

37. Where is Brian Boru buried?

38. Who was the Protestant barrister who "hated the very name of England," was a champion of religious freedom and Irish independence and a revolutionary who led an invasion of Ireland from France?

39. Whose body was secretly buried in quicklime after he was executed during the Easter Rising?

40. Who introduced the potato to Ireland?

41. Who invented the submarine?

42. When was the Land League founded, and by whom?

43. Who coined the phrase "Ulster will fight, and Ulster will be right"?

44. Who was known as "The Dove of the Church"?

45. Who was the first undisputed high king of Ireland?

46. Who proclaimed himself king of Ireland in 1541?

47. Who founded Trinity College in 1591?

48. Who was the leader of the Wild Geese?

49. Who said "When my country takes her place among the nations of the earth, then, not til then, let my

epitaph be written"?

50. When was the Gaelic Athletic Association formed?

51. What newspaper did Thomas Davis and Charles Duffy found in 1842?

52. How did the word "boycott" come into use?

53. Who founded the Gaelic League in 1893?

54. Who formed the Irish Transport and General Workers' Union in 1909?

55. What was the "Golden Age" of Ireland?

56. Name the Irish Jew who captured world-wide attention when he was elected lord mayor of Dublin.

57. What did the Act of Union in 1800 do?

58. What affect did the Wyndham Act of 1903 have on land ownership?

59. What were the Statutes of Kilkenny?

60. According to W.B. Yeats, what were the four tragic moments in Irish history?

61. Who was the first Irish prisoner to go "on the blanket" in March 1976?

62. Who was the first president of Ireland, and where was he born?

63. Who said, "Ireland unfree shall never be at peace"?

64. What was the name of the boat that landed weapons at Howth in 1914 to arm the Irish Volunteers?

65. Name the two leaders in the Battle of the Boyne in 1690.

66. Who was Sean MacBride's mother?

67. Who was the first leader of the *Clann na Poblachta* (Republican Family Party)?

68. How many Irish enlisted in the British Armed Forces in World War II?

69. Who were known as the "Blue Shirts"?

70. What did the Sinn Fein and the IRA do to DeValera in 1925?

71. What does *Fianna Fáil* mean?

72. Who founded the Fianna Fáil?

73. What color caps did the Black and Tans wear?

74. What did the Irish Volunteers become?

75. Who was called the "Scarlet Pimpernel" of Irish nationalism?

76. Who was acting president of the Dáil in 1919?

77. Who was elected president of the Dáil in 1919?

78. Who arranged Eamon de Valera's escape from jail in 1919?

79. What party won the election in 1918?

80. Where was de Valera during the Easter uprising?

81. What two groups made up the rebel forces of the Easter Rising in 1916?

82. How long did the Easter Rising last?

83. How many rebels did the Irish Free State execute in the Civil War?

84. Who introduced the tricolor flag in 1848?

85. In the general elections of 1918, whose campaign slogan read, "Put Him In To Get Him Out ... Vote For ... The Man In Jail For Ireland"?

86. Who seized the Four Courts in Dublin in 1922?

87. Which prime minister of England negotiated the treaty with Ireland in 1922?

88. What incident started the Irish Civil War in 1922?

89. How long did England occupy Ireland?

90. What did St. Patrick first come to Ireland as?

91. When was Ireland first inhabited?

92. When was the Home Rule Bill creating Northern Ireland passed?

93. What political party did Arthur Griffith establish in 1900?

94. Who was the first president of the National Land League?

95. Who had a nickname of "Swaggering Dan"?

96. Where did Brian Boru defeat the Norsemen?

97. Who said, "Human blood is no cement for the temple of liberty"?

98. What was the population of Ireland prior to the Famine of 1845?

99. The Penal Laws passed in the early seventeen hundreds had what effect on education?

100. Who wrote, "All government without consent of the governed is the very essence of slavery"?

101. After the Battle of the Boyne in 1690, how many acres of land did Catholics lose?

102. What year did the Earl of Pembroke lead the Anglo-Norman invasion of Ireland?

103. Who formed the Irish Citizen's Army?

104. Where were the rebels of 1916 executed?

105. Who described the Uprising of 1916 as "the year one in Irish history and Irish life"?

106. When did the Normans come to Ireland?

107. What was the purpose of Celtic crosses?

108. What does *Sinn Fein* mean?

109. What group killed the British chief secretary in 1882?

110. During the famine of 1845-1849, where did most of Ireland's crops go?

111. What is *phytophthera infertans*?

112. What did Daniel O'Connell and Charles Parnell have in common?

113. What is Long Kesh Prison known as?

114. What was Ireland's position in World War II?

115. How long was Dublin Castle the seat of British rule in Ireland?

116. Where was Daniel O'Connell's heart buried?

117. Where did Daniel O'Connell come from?

118. How many representatives did Ireland have in the Westminister Parliament in 1800?

119. Who were described as "pioneers in apartheid colonialism"?

120. When did the bubonic plague ("Black Death") hit Ireland?

121. What was the purpose of the Penal Laws passed in the 18th century?

122. Where did Cromwell force the Irish aristocracy to move?

123. Who said that the rights of property took priority over the Irish peasant's right to survive?

124. Who was described as a "souper" during the Famine?

125. How many people fled Ireland during the Famine?

126. Approximately how many people died during the Potato Famine?

127. Who started the first church building program in Ireland?

128. Where did Charles Parnell die?

129. Who replaced the Home Rule League with the Irish National League?

130. Who founded the Irish Republican Brotherhood?

131. What does the white in the flag of Ireland represent?

132. What does the green represent in the flag of Ireland?

133. What does the orange in the flag of Ireland represent?

134. How many women were in the rebel force in Dublin on Easter Monday, 1916?

135. What was the name of the German ship that sunk on Good Friday in 1916 off the coast of Munster?

136. Who were the West Britons?

137. What did the Gaelic Athletic Association ban?

138. What did the Irish Volunteers become?

139. At the battle of the Boyne, who led the Catholic forces?

140. What was the ethnic make-up of the forces commanded by James II at the Battle of the Boyne?

141. Where is the tomb of Strongbow, Earl of Pembroke, located?

142. When was Ireland constitutionally absorbed into England?

143. Cork was formerly a religious settlement founded by what saint?

144. Who built the walls in Cork?

145. What caused the deforestation of Ireland?

146. What was the Hill of Tara?

147. In 1649, who led the slaughter of Irish woman, children, non-combatants and captives?

148. After Cromwell, approximately what percentage of land was transferred from Catholics to Protestants?

149. When was the oath to the British Crown abolished?

150. When was the Irish Constitution adopted?

151. Who was Douglas Hyde?

152. Patrick Pearse, Thomas MacDonagh and Joseph Plunkett were members of what council in 1914?

153. What action did members of Sinn Fein take after their election to Westminister in the early 1900's?

154. What new status was given Ireland in the Anglo-Irish Treaty of 1921?

155. What was the most objectionable part of the Anglo-Irish Treaty of 1921?

156. What did the Ballot Act of 1872 introduce?

157. In the early 1900's what were the three major industries of Dublin?

158. What was *Saor Eire*?

159. What was the purpose of the Gaelic League?

160. What did Sir Edward Carson, Captain James Craig and Bonar Law have in common?

161. From what country did the Ulster Volunteer Forces receive some of its arms in 1914 from outside of Great Britain?

162. Who led the First Nationalists at Westminister during World War I?

163. Who constituted the Nac Irish Volunteers?

164. Who were the Fenians?

165. What were the Manchester martyrs executed for in 1867?

166. Who was Ms. Katherine O'Shea?

167. The first railway line was between Dublin and Kingstown. How long was it?

168. Who led an abortive insurrection of United Irishmen in 1803?

169. In 1841 there were some 300,000 holdings of five acres of farmland. How many were there in 1851?

170. Who proposed the Irish Land Act of 1870?

171. The Irish Land League was founded in 1879 by a young man from Mayo. Who was he?

172. What is the only surviving major public building from the 17th century in Ireland?

173. What is the oldest bridge crossing the Liffey?

174. Where did the *S.S. Lusitania* sink?

175. Who said "Educate that you might be free"?

176. What year did Ireland first compete in the Olympics as a separate nation?

177. Who founded the Irish Christian Brothers?

178. What did Ptolemy call Dublin in 140 AD?

179. What did the Romans call Ireland?

180. Who opened the first movie house in Ireland, the "Volta", in 1909?

181. Who gave the City of Galway its charter?

182. What was the Uprising of 1848 known as?

183. Who won the Battle of the Yellow Ford in 1598?

184. What did Australian explorer Douglas Mawson take to the South Pole in 1908?

185. Who said "We serve neither King nor Kaiser - but Ireland"?

186. Who said, "All through our colonial battle against the British, the Irish freedom struggle was my greatest inspiration"?

187. What does "Beyond the Pale" mean?

188. Who declared Ireland a republic?

189. Who did Winston Churchill refer to as "that damned Englishman"?

190. When did Ireland join the Common Market?

191. What was Countess Markiewicz's maiden name?

192. Who was the "Maeve of the Irish Volunteers" in 1915?

193. What did Hobart's Catholic Relief Bill give Catholics in 1793?

194. Where was Countess Markiewicz during the Easter Rising?

195. What was known as famine food?

196. Builders of the Erie Canal advertised in Belfast, Cork, and Dublin papers for laborers to come to America. What was the salary range offered?

197. What was the New York City point of entry for Irish immigrants before Ellis Island was built?

198. Why was Daniel O'Connell denied his seat in Parliament?

199. Who are referred to as "planters"?

200. A young doctor returned to Laos after he was discharged from the Navy — founded MEDICO and helped establish several clinics and hospitals. He was an Irish Albert Schweitzer who unfortunately died at age 34. Who was he?

201. When and what was the first book printed in Ireland?

202. The major period of immigration from Ireland to America took place during which three decades?

203. What is the name of the prison in Dublin where many Fenians were kept in the 1800's?

204. Name the first Catholic college for higher studies in Ireland.

205. What does Article II of the Irish Constitution state?

206. How did Wood Quay in Dublin get its name?

207. What is the Presbyterian equivalent of the Whiteboys?

ARTS & LITERATURE

1. What rebel song does Sean O'Farrell appear in?

2. Who wrote "A Nation Once Again"?

3. Who wrote "The Last Rose of Summer"?

4. What Irish rock band made their debut in America with the hit "New Year's Day"?

5. What was the first successful Celtic rock group?

6. What is a fleadh?

7. What was the Public Dance Hall Act?

8. Who did the soundtrack for the film *Barry Lyndon?*

9. Who wrote *Four Green Fields?*

10. Who formed the group, Ceoltóirí Chualann?

35

11. Who was the first major American composer of classical music?

12. What is the oldest form of Irish dance music?

13. Who gave the order to "hang the harpers wherever found"?

14. Whose collection of Irish dance music is called *Where the Shannon Rises*?

15. What is the "bible of Irish traditional music"?

16. Whose collection entitled *Old Irish Folk Music and Songs* appeared in 1909?

17. Name the first serious collection of traditional melodies of Ireland.

18. What was the famous festival of 1792 that brought together the music of 18th century itinerant harp players?

19. Who wrote a poem about "The Fiddler of Dooney"?

20. Who was Blind Raferty?

21. What is Jim Crow?

22. What are Irish drums called, and what are the made of?

23. Who wrote "Spancihill"?

24. Who was known as the "Donegal Piper"?

25. What are uillean pipes?

26. Who wrote a song about the Lisdoon-varna Music Festival?

27. What song has this verse?
    Grey said victory was sure
    Soon the firebrand he'd secure
    Until he met at Glenmalure
    With Feach McHugh O'Byrne.

28. Who were the four popular Sligo fid-dlers who settled in New York in the 1920s?

29. What is *Comhaltas Ceolteoiri Eire-ann*?

30. Who was the female vocalist for Skara Brae, the Bothy Band, and Touch-stone?

31. Who was "Another martyr for old Ireland/Another murder for the crown"?

32. Who was Joe Heaney?

33. What is Willie Clancy Week?

34. What is Elvis Costello's real name?

35. Who is called "Ireland's National Composer"?

36. Which city is referred to in "The Town I Love So Well"?

37. Who was John Field?

38. Who is generally recognized as the greatest living Irish tenor?

39. Who is the leader of the Chieftans?

40. What was the name of "The Wild Colonial Boy"?

41. What is pop singer Boy George's full name?

42. Who were the Flanagan Brothers?

43. What Belfast musician recorded "Moondance"?

44. Who was the singer for the Dubliners who died in 1984?

45. Who founded the *Irish Review*?

46. The National Theatre Society and Yeats Irish Literary Theatre merged. What resulted from the merger?

47. Who wrote the poem "When You Are Old"?

48. Three Irishmen have won the Noble Prize for Literature. Who are they?

49. Who wrote *Hidden Ireland*?

50. Who wrote *An Intimate Portrait of Sean O'Casey*?

51. Who said, "I have a total irreverence for anything connected with society, except that which makes the road safer, the beer stronger, the old men

and women warmer in the winter and happier in the summer"?

52. Who said, "To get drunk in the depression was a victory"?

53. What was Brendan Behan's autobiography entitled?

54. What woman was instrumental in the founding of the Abbey Theatre?

55. Who wrote the songs "Kelly of Killaine" and "Boolavogue"?

56. What Irish author described himself: as "A man of small virtue, inclined to extravagance and alcoholism"?

57. James Joyce as a young boy lived on North Richmond Street in Dublin. What was the number?

58. "Don't make a hero out of me. I'm only a simple, middle-class man" — a self-portrait of which Irish author?

59. James Joyce graduated from college in 1902. What was the name of the college?

60. James Joyce only dedicated one of his works to someone. Who?

61. "For you see, in Ireland there is no future, only the past happening over and over." In what book is this the last line?

62. When Ernest Hemingway met James Joyce, he gave him a letter of introduction. Who signed the letter?

63. At the time of Joyce's death there were two books on his desk: one was a Greek lexicon. What was the name of the other book?

64. How many brothers and sisters did James Joyce have?

65. Who taught a course about James Joyce at Belvedere College?

66. What song has the chorus line "Glory O! Glory O! to the bold Fenian men "

67. Whose epitaph reads: "Cast a cold eye on life, on death. Horsemen, pass by"?

68. Who wrote the Irish National Anthem, "A Soldier's Song"?

69. Who was popularly known as "AE"?

70. How many plays written by George Bernard Shaw have Ireland as a subject?

71. What was John Synge's most famous play?

72. Who was the model for Buck Mulligan of *Ulysses*?

73. What is the *Book of Kells*?

74. When was the Abbey Theatre founded?

75. Who wrote *The Wind Among the Reed* in 1899?

76. Who was Richard Castle?

77. What is Ireland's foremost example of Palladianism?

78. Who designed Castletown?

79. Who was called "The King of the Pipers"?

80. Who wrote "Caitlin Mavourneen"?

81. Who was Finley Peter Dunne's alter ego?

82. Who wrote "When Irish Eyes Are Smiling" and "Mother Machree"?

83. Who wrote the ballad "Roddy Mc-Corley"?

84. In what song does Fergal O'Hanlon die?

85. Whose novels contain the Phelans, an Irish-American family from Albany?

86. Who wrote *Children of the Dead End*?

87. When was *Ulysses* published?

88. Who wrote the play *Translations*?

89. Who wrote the *Year of the French*?

90. Who wrote *Recollection of an Irish Rebel*?

91. Who was the first American Irishman to become a major novelist?

92. Who wrote *The Midnight Court*?

93. Gypo Nolan is the main character in what famous novel/movie?

94. Which Beckett play featured two tramps, Estragon and Nadimir?

95. Who lived at Number Seven Eccles Street, Dublin?

96. Who described Ireland as "the sow that eats her own furrow"?

97. Who said "Ireland, sir, is like no other place under heaven"?

98. Who said, "For where there are Irish there's loving and fighting. And when we stop either its Ireland no more"?

99. Who said "We are the greatest talkers since the Greeks"?

100. Where did the quote "Shakespeare-isn't he the one who writes like Synge?" appear?

101. Who created *Dracula*?

102. Who wrote *Traits and Stories of the Irish Peasantry*?

103. Who did Newsweek magazine call "a worthy successor to W.B. Yeats"?

104. What was Frank O'Connor's real name?

105. Who said: "I would rather be burned at the stake by Irish Catholics than protected by Englishmen"?

106.   Where was Liam O'Flaherty born?

107.   Who wrote *The Hostage*?

108.   When is Bloomsday?

109.   What were Brian O'Nolan's pen names?

110.   Who wrote *Memories of A Catholic Girlhood?*

111.   Who wrote the following verse?
       My country is a Kiltartan cross,
       My countrymen Kiltartan's poor,
       No likely end could bring them loss
       Or leave them happier than before.

112.   Which Liam O'Flaherty novel was made into a movie and won for the director an Academy Award?

113.   Who wrote *Knocknagow,* perhaps the most famous of all 19th century Irish books?

114.   One portrayed the Irish as raucous, drunken boyo's and dreamers, the other as dapper, charming men whose wisecracks delighted audiences. Who were these famous Irish playwrights?

115.   Who were the Irish immigrants' equivalent of Lerner & Lowe who wrote, produced and acted in their "knock-down and slambang plays to the delight of their predominantly Irish audiences"?

116. Who was the Irish immigrant's poet laureate?

117. Who wrote the poem "The Toome Road"?

118. Who wrote *Letters of An Irish Publican*?

119. Whose collection of poetry in entitled *Missouri Sequence*?

120. Who wrote a collection of poetry entitled *North*?

121. Whose autobiography is entitled *The Price of My Soul*?

122. What was Samuel Beckett's first book, written in 1931?

123. What song has this verse?
     For the great Gaels of Ireland
     Are the men that God made mad,
     For all their wars are merry,
     And all their songs are sad.

124. Who wrote *Blacklist Section H*?

125. Who wrote *The Lonely Passion of Judith Hearne*?

126. Who wrote *The Drapier Letters*, a protest against England's control of Ireland's monetary system?

127. Complete this verse:
     Then drill, my Paddies, drill
     Drill, my heroes drill,
     Drill all day, no sugar in your tay,
     Working on the . . . .

128. Who is Seamus Murphy?

129. Who wrote the poem "The Bells of Shandon"?

130. Who wrote *The Riddle of The Sands*?

131. Who wrote *Gulliver's Travels*?

132. Who wrote *Faragan's Retreat*?

133. Who wrote the play *DA*?

134. What song has these lines?
     So the old flute was doomed
     And its fate was pathetic
     'Twas fostened and burned
     At the stake as heretic.
     While the flames roared around it
     They heard a strange noise
     Twas the old flute still whistling
     "The Protestant Boys."

135. What song has these lines?
     She died of a fever
     And none could relieve her
     And that was the end
     Of Sweet Mollie Malone.

136. In what saga does Cu Chulainn single-handedly defend Ulster during a Southern Irish invasion?

137. Who said "All good women are manly, and all good men are womanly"?

IRELAND-TODAY

1. Name the Irish ministers involved in the arms trial of 1970 in Dublin.

2. Who said "...the Irish Government can no longer stand by and see innocent people injured and perhaps worse"?

3. In Ireland, who is known as "The Boss"?

4. What is the Green Cross?

5. Who said, "So long as Britain pursues the phantom of military victory over the IRA, the violence will continue and the search for peace will be in vain"?

6. What is the political goal of Sinn Fein?

7. What happened at Burntollet Bridge on January 4, 1969?

8. Who is the leader of the Irish Labor Party?

9. What is known as the Oak Leaf County?

47

10. Who is Douglas Hurd?

11. What is the name of Ireland's current affairs magazine?

12. Who is the President of Ireland?

13. What is the name of the new Irish language newspaper published in Ireland?

14. Who played in the 1984 All-Ireland hurling final?

15. Who is the leader of the Social Democratic and Labor Party (SDLP)?

16. What percentage of the Irish population have red hair?

17. What is a Supergrass?

18. What is the oldest licensed pub in Dublin?

19. Who did Polish leader Lech Walesa express solidarity with in 1981?

20. Where was the Northern Ireland Parliament located before it was abolished in 1972?

21. What is *Aosdana*?

22. Who is the host of "The Late Late Show" on RTE?

23. When was the Diplock system instituted in Northern Ireland?

24. Where is the island known as St. Patrick's Purgatory?

25. Is divorce legal in Ireland?

26. Who was just appointed Archbishop of Dublin?

27. Who does "Ireland's Silent Service" refer to?

28. What is the Irish airline called?

29. Name the Minister for Justice.

30. Name the Irish Minister for Foreign Affairs.

31. Where is the Connemara Pony Show held annually?

32. When was the Abbey Theater founded?

33. Who is the patron saint of Dublin?

34. What is *Bord Failte Eireann*?

35. Where is Vinegar Hill?

36. What happened to Nelson's Pillar?

37. Which country recently developed a scientific method for teaching the Irish language?

38. What was O'Connell Bridge in Dublin formerly called?

39. Name the Irishman elected President of the U.N. General Assembly in 1960

40. What does *Erin Go Bragh* mean?

41. Whose seat for British Parliament did Bobby Sands win in a by-election?

42. What is the Flags and Emblem Act of 1954?

43. Who said "We are too small to be apart or for the border to be there for all time"?

44. What did plastic bullets replace?

45. What is the Gardai?

46. Whose visit to Ireland in 1979 spawned the largest open-air Mass ever held in Ireland?

47. What city is 800 years old in 1985?

48. When did the National Gallery of Ireland Open?

49. What did the Irish pound drop to in 1984 in American money?

50. What was the first book to be "unbanned" by the Irish Government?

51. What percentage of the Irish workforce arrives to work on a bicycle?

52. What is the time difference between Dublin and Boston?

53. Who sponsored the "mother and child health scheme" in 1951?

54. What are the four national morning papers?

55. Who from Northern Ireland won the Nobel Peace Prize?

IRISH-AMERICAN

1. What river is dyed green each year on March 17?

2. Where is John F. Kennedy's ancestral home?

3. What American city has a section called the "Irish Channel"?

4. In the 19th century, what Irish-built structure was called the "eighth wonder of the world"?

5. Who coined the phrase "Manifest Destiny"?

6. Who was the father of Labor Day in America?

7. What was known as the "Broadway Valhalla"?

8. Who was Thomas Taggart?

9. Where did the "Molly Maquires" originate?

10. What Irish-American politician was called "the Last of the Bosses"?

11. Who is the head of Heinz International?

12. What is Carlow College in Pittsburgh, PA named after?

13. What ship sank off the coast of Massachusetts in 1849, killing 99 Irish who were fleeing the Famine?

14. Who was the first Irish-American mayor of San Francisco?

15. Which state has the largest proportion of Irish-Americans?

16. What American company is drilling for oil in the Celtic Sea?

17. According to recent statistics, what percentage of corporate America is presently controlled by Irish-Americans?

18. Who was the first Irish-American Olympic medalist in modern times?

19. Name the two Irish-American, male finalists in the 1984 Wimbledon tennis match.

20. What is the Dearie Resolution?

21. What film did Walt Disney make about Ireland?

22. Where was *The Quiet Man* filmed, and who were the leading stars?

23. Which state has the most Irish descendants?

24. Who was the first International President of the Teamsters Union?

25. What college in 1984 dedicated its new library to Tip O'Neill?

26. Who was known as "Meagher of the Sword" in the Civil War?

27. Who directed the movie, *The Informer,* based on Liam O'Flaherty's novel?

28. What movie star of Irish ancestry plans to star in a movie as Michael Collins?

29. What Irish-American group gives grants to causes of peace, culture, and charity in Ireland?

30. Where is "The Irish Wilderness" in America?

31. Who is the head of the Irish-American Unity Conference?

32. Name the well-loved Irish vocalist who made her debut on "The Arthur Godfrey Show" in the 1950s.

33. Who was grand marshall of the 1983 New York City Parade?

34. Who recently won the Pulitzer Prize for his fictional portrayal of Irish-Americans in Albany, NY?

35. Who was responsible for building St. Patrick's Cathedral in New York City?

36. Who was Typhoid Mary?

37. Which family has run Albany, NY for most of this century?

38. Where was the *Shamrock,* the first Irish-American newspaper, published?

39. Who did John Devoy call "the meanest man who ever filled the office of President of the United States"?

40. Who wrote *The Irish Immigrants' Guide to the United States* in the mid-19th century?

41. Who printed the first copies of the American Declaration of Independence?

42. What was Ulysses Grant's Irish connection?

43. When did the first St. Patrick's Day Parade take place in New York City?

44. Who were the "San Patricos"?

45. Who is known as the "Purple Shamrock"?

46. Which Irish visitor said, "I have nothing to declare except my genius," upon arriving in New York?

47. What famous American helped select the site of Shannon Airport in 1930?

48. Who was the famous editor of *The Pilot* from 1869 to 1890?

49. Who said, "What good is it to be Irish if you don't know that the world will eventually break your heart"?

50. What urban area has the largest number of Irish Americans?

51. Who are the "Four Horsemen" of American politics?

52. Who was the first Irish-American Catholic to hold a cabinet office in the United States?

53. Who was hailed as the "Queen of the Populists" among the mid-western Irish settlers?

54. Who wants to "retire to the west of Ireland and write novels"?

55. Where was Irish coffee invented?

56. How many cases of Irish whiskey were consumed in the USA in 1982?

57. Who is the head of the California Labor Federation?

58. Who led the Chilean revolt against Spain in 1814?

59. The Plough and the Stars is the emblem of what movement?

60. What American Indian tribe's language has a number of words similar to ancient Celtic both in spelling and meaning?

61. Who sailed a curragh from Dingle, Kerry to Boston, MA in 1978 to re-create St. Brendan's voyage?

62. Where has Ogham, the ancient Irish script, been discovered in America?

63. How many Irishmen died at the Alamo?

64. What was the *Celtic Monthly*?

65. At Bishop Hughes' suggestion, the Irish Emigrant Society founded its own bank. It is still in business — one of the largest savings and loan banks in the nation. What is its name?

66. Where were Irish slaves initially shipped after the Cromwellian conquests of Ireland?

67. What was the famous section of New York City where the Irish lived during the mid-19th century?

68. Who wrote the autobiography, *I'd Do It Again*?

69. What was Colonel William Cody's nickname?

70. What American opened a sports car factory in Belfast that eventually went bankrupt?

71. Who said, "As a candidate for President of the United States, I call on all members of the Rainbow Coalition to work actively for the withdrawal of English troops from Irish territory"?

72. Who is the leader of the Irish National Caucus?

73. Who were the Celtic Players?

74. Who wrote *Gone With The Wind*?

75. What airline services Belfast to New York and back?

76. Who is the current American ambassador to Ireland?

77. Where were Andrew Jackson's parents from?

78. Who wrote *I'll Come Back in the Springtime,* the story of President Kennedy's visit to Ireland in 1963?

79. Who was Mother Jones?

80. Where was Henry Ford's first car factory outside the United States?

81. A man from Mayo—forever champion of the poor—he rose from a spare parts clerk to president of the NY City Council. Who is he?

82. Who was called the greatest Irish-American composer of light operas?

83. What caused the Broad Street riot in Boston in 1837?

84. Who was called, "The Apostle of Temperance"?

85. Name the political nativist party opposed to Irish Catholics entering America in the 19th century.

86. Name the Japanese ship that sank Kennedy's PT109 during WW II.

87. Who was the first Irish policeman in Boston?

88. Who was the Irish spy hired by Pinkerton to infiltrate the Molly Maguires?

89. What famous canal built by the Irish was called Clinton's Ditch?

90. What city had the largest number of Irish immigrants in the South?

91. How many Irish died in the Boston cholera epidemic in 1849?

92. Who was the first Archbishop of New York?

93. Who was America's first Congressional Medal of Honor winner in WW II?

94. What was the famous Irish battalion during the American Civil War?

95. Who wrote *It's The Irish*?

96. Who wrote *Profiles in Courage*?

97. Who created "Mr. Dooley"?

98. Who was Tyrone Power's great-grandfather?

99. How many St. Patrick's Day Parades are celebrated in the U.S.A.?

100. What is an "Ethiopean delineator"?

101. What were the Astor Riots of 1848?

102. What famous play about an Irish girl and a Jewish boy ran a record 2,327 performances on Broadway in the 1920's?

103. Name the Irish millionaire who had a set of jewelry for each day of the month.

104. Whose giant mural "Finnigan's Sleep" hangs in the Black Rose Pub in Boston?

105. Who was Elizabeth Gurley Flynn?

106. Who was Billy the Kid?

107. What is TV host Mike Douglas' real name?

108. Whose autobiography was called *The Wind At My Back*?

109. Who was Hercules Mulligan?

110. What is "St. Patrick's on the Lizard"?

111. What is the name of the Irish American who rebuilt Dromoland Castle?

112. Where were the Irish taxed for being Irish?

113. What is characteristic of "Lace Curtain Irish"?

114. An Irishwoman was hanged as a witch in Boston in 1688. Who condemned her in a sermon at the Old North Church?

115. Lord Baltimore named a large part of Maryland "New Ireland." It was divided into three parts. Name them.

116. What percent of the population of America was Irish in 1790?

117. At the Battle of Bunker Hill, 54 Americans were killed. How many were natives of Ireland?

118. What message did Al Smith send to the Pope after his defeat in 1928?

119. Who was the most decorated chaplain in United States military history?

120. Who were the "Wild Geese"?

121. What were the "Kitchen Rackets"?

122. Who was the first Catholic Bishop in the United States?

123. Who was the "Gentleman from Ton" who introduced grand opera to the United States?

124. The Society of Tammany, founded in 1889, was the beginning of a powerful political organization that helped the Irish in New York. Whom does the name honor?

125. Who was the grande dame of American Society who made White Sulphur Springs the first fashionable resort in the 1860's?

126. What did Charles Carroll and Thomas Fitzsimmons have in common?

127. Why is Evacuation Day—March 17th —a legal holiday in Boston?

128. Who was the "Father of the American Navy"?

129. Why did the American Irish join fraternal organizations such as the Ancient Order of Hibernians?

130. What famous New York City landmark is located on the site of the Old Irish Shantytown?

131. Who was the Irish pioneer who guided the first wagon train across the plains to California and later taught Kit Carson frontier survival skills?

132. 1853...The nuns and 60 pupils fled...the superior cried, "The Bishop has twenty thousand Irishmen at his command in Boston!" What was the event?

133. "Independent in everything—mutual in nothing" was the motto of a newspaper founded by Mike Walsh, a spokesman for impoverished Irish laborers. What was the name of the paper?

134. An Irishman on the West Coast who built San Francisco's first gas lighting system, established an iron foundry, organized the San Jose railroad, built a mansion in San Francisco and then gave his wife the "ultimate gift," a Cinderella coach made of glass —who was he?

135. Who was the American heavyweight champion in 1853? Born in Tipperary,

he settled in Troy, NY and later became a congessman. He also founded the first fashionable gambling saloon in America at Saratoga Springs.

136. In the elections of 1854, voters in what state elected the highest number of "know-nothing," anti-Catholic, anti-Irish candidates?

137. What was the name of the famous regiment first led by Col. Michael Corcoran which fought with "conspicuous bravery" at the Battle of Bull Run, Antietam, and in many battles since then?

138. Who was the first American president to accord the Irish national political recognition by appointing John O'Sullivan minister to Portugal?

139. During the Civil War thousands of Irishmen volunteered to fight. How many union regiments had the word "Irish" in their name?

140. Who were the two leading liberal clergymen of the late 19th century who encouraged Irishmen to become part of American life—much to the disliking of some of their confreres?

141. Quinn
Pat Quinn
C. Patrick Quinn
Col. Cornelius Patrick Quinn
Col. C. P. Quinn
Patrick Quinn
Pat Quinn
Old Quinn
—of whom is this an autobiographical sketch?

142. Peter O'Reilly and Patrick McLaughlin, miners, followed the lure of gold from California to Nevada. There, they were puzzled by the "heavy black stuff" mixed with the gold. What had they discovered?

143. The first American cardinal was an Irishman. What was his name?

144. Who was the "Hombre de Verdad" who maintained law and order on the Texas/Mexican border, brought cattle rustling under control, put an end to mob lynchings, and is remembered as "the exemplar of all Irish law-and-order men"?

145. "He fell without loss of reputation among the bulk of his supporters...the poor of this city. [They revere him as] the victim of rich men's malice...a friend of the poor who used public funds to make work for the poor...$50,000 given to charity ...free coal in winter, free beer in summer"—was a eulogy for whom?

146. The Irish dominated which two sports in the first half of the 19th century?

147. Who was "Boston's strong boy" who, at 5' 10½" and 190 lbs., could "lick any sonofabitch alive...if any of 'em here doubts it, come on!"?

148. What was one of John L. Sullivan's major contributions to prizefighting?

149. John L. Sullivan's longest match was fought against Jake Kilrain. How long was the match, and how many rounds did it last?

150. Who won the heavyweight champsionship title from Sullivan?

151. How did John L. Sullivan round out his career?

152. What does the term "hyphenated Americans" refer to?

153. Who was New York City's first Irish Catholic mayor?

154. He arrived from Co. Roscommon with $10 in his pocket, opened Los Angeles' first drugstore, and was elected governor of California 13 years after he arrived in the state—who is he?

155. Who said, "If you doubt the value of an education, ask the man who never had one"? Then, as governor, he signed the largest school appropriation bill to date.

156. Which politician made the Brown Derby famous?

157. Who was the Irish parliamentarian who championed the cause of Independence, toured the United States in 1880, and addressed the House of Representatives? He raised $350,000 and helped organize the American Land League to support the struggle "at home".

158. What was General McAuliffe's reply when the Germans demanded his surrender at Bastogne?

159. 1913—A landmark year for two of the most famous Irish politicians: one was

elected speaker of the New York Assembly, the other was elected mayor
of Boston. Who are they?

160. What were the three organizations
which helped Irish immigrants merge
into the American national life?

161. "Hinky Dink" McKenna, "Bathhouse
John" Coughlin, Pat Nash, Ed Kelly,
Tom Pendergast, Frank Hague, Ber-
nie McFeely, and the O'Connells—what did they have in common?

162. Margaret Tobin Brown, a grande
dame of international society, was on
the Titanic when it went down. She
kept the spirits of her lifeboat
companions up by the "force of her
will," rowing until her hands bled,
telling jokes, singing arias from the
grand operas, and burying her own
fear. Her bravery earned her what title?

163. "Big Tim" Sullivan, state senator from
the Bowery (1893-1913), supported
women's suffrage and cast the
deciding vote limiting the woman's
work week to how many hours?

164. What was the Sullivan Law, pro-
hibiting the carrying of concealed
weapons, originally used for?

165. The Irish skill in creating ethnic coalitions helped them on two fronts. What
were they?

166. Dooley and Hennessy are two charac-
ters created by one of the greatest

American satirists. Name him.

167. What was the life expectancy of an Irishman who came to Boston in 1850?

168. F. Scott Fitzgerald's grandfather, Mc-Quillan, and Eugene O'Neill's granfather, Quinlan, were in the same line of business—one that Irish immigrants entered because it did not require a large capital outlay. What was it?

169. What was one of the major, longlasting effects of Alfred E. Smith's presidential campaign?

170. *Up From The City Streets* was a biography of whom?

171. October 19, 1919—Governor Smith appeared at Carnegie Hall to debate a leading newspaper publisher who had accused him of fixing the price of milk and being insensitive to the effects of the high cost of milk on the poor. The publisher failed to show up. Smith defended his policies by debating himself and answering all charges before an overflow crowd. Who was the publisher?

172. Besides bigotry, what two factors contributed to Smith's defeat?

173. "Gangplank Bill" was the irreverent nickname for which prelate of the Church?

174. Who founded the Tammany Club?

175. "He did it for a friend."—i.e., took a civil service exam, served 60 days for

fraud, and was elected alderman while serving his sentence. This refers to whom?

176. Who said, "My mother toiled as a scrubwoman...I told the scrubwoman cleaning the corridors of the city hall to 'get up.' "?

177. "A Bigger, Better, and Busier Boston" was the campaign slogan for whom?

178. Who was the first American born of Irish parents to be elected Mayor of Boston?

179. Most rank and file Democrats, particularly those from Massachusetts, supported the renomination of Alfred E. Smith in 1931, except James M. Curley. He renamed himself Jaime Miguel Curleo and arranged to be an alternate delegate from what territory so he could support Roosevelt?

180. Which two Irish writers of the late 19th century were the reputed spokesmen for the immigrants of their race?

181. Who was the first Irish governor of Massachusetts?

182. He ruled the political scene for over 30 years. His net estate was $3,768 —not even enough to cover his bequests. Who is he?

183. How many American presidents have visited Ireland while in office?

184. "He had the Irish gift for turning language into something iridescent and surprising." Whom does this refer to?

185. Which governor of New York, while addressing the legislature, referred to himself as a graduate of the Fulton Fish Market?

186. A hard-drinking Irishman...quick to take offense...carrying a chip on his shoulder...a dapper-social climber —what does this describe?

187. Which Irish novelist wore a mock Phi Beta Kappa with "Nope" engraved on it—a tribute to the years he wished he had spent at Yale?

188. Faulkner wrote about Yoknapataupha country. Fitzgerald wrote about the Riviera. Where did James Farrell write about?

189. Who was the first Irish Catholic head of Tammany Hall?

190. James T. Farrell's best novels were sets of three and four volumes respectively. What were they entitled?

191. What city attempted to have Farrell's *Studs Lonigan* banned in 1948?

192. The first serious, well-recognized American playwright was an Irishman. Who was he?

193. Who was the singer who reflected the patriotism of first and second generation Irish Americans?

194. Who wrote "Over There"?

195. What were the themes of many of O'Neill's plays and novels?

196. Name the Irishman who was the leading photographer during the Civil War.

197. Who designed the White House?

198. Who was the first American woman to walk in space?

199. Who did the English refer to as the "Wild Irishman" when they were colonizing America?

200. Who demanded, "Be more Irish than Harvard"?

201. Who was the "Radio Priest" who broadcasted controversial radio programs on politics and religion from 1928-1936?

202. Who were the Irish actor and actress who made dramatic comebacks on the broadway stage in 1945—one as the star of the *Glass Managerie,* the other in *Harvey*?

203. Who was the first Irish mayor of Boston?

204. What secret society, formed in 1834, included in its program "agitation for Irish freedom, ardent support of the Church and the stimulation of interest in Irish history, culture and folklore"?

205. Who is the president of Inn American which owns hotels in eight cities?

206. A champion of social justice who could "cut through a municipal budget" like a banker while maintaining the "other-worldly air of a modern St. Francis"—describes a politician from Detroit. Who was he?

207. "My dear Joe," Roosevelt wrote. "You have maintained your justly earned reputation of being a two-fisted, hard-hitting executive." He was rewarded by an appointment to the court of St. James—the first Irish Catholic to ever hold that post. "Joe" refers to whom?

208. Few Irishmen had been appointed to important places in executive and judicial branches of the federal government until whose presidency?

209. A likeable Irish politician...a workaholic with a genius for organizing constituent support...the first in a long line of Irish Catholic chairmen of the National Democratic Party —which New York politician does this describe?

210. Franklin Roosevelt's two favorite Republicans were an Irishman from Oklahoma (Secretary of War under Hoover) and a World War I hero (federal prosecutor from western New York and head of the Office of Strategic Services, also under Hoover). What were their names?

211. Which president enraged Irish Americans by referring to hyphenated Americans—"Irishmen whose hearts had not crossed the Atlantic" —while dedicating a monument to Commodore John Berry?

212. FDR invited a renowned Irish Catholic priest to pronounce benediction at the close of his inauguration in January, 1938. The priest was selected in recognition of his outstanding achievements in the field of social justice (and his support of FDR). This was the first inauguration to have a benediction as well as an invocation. Who was this Minnesotan priest?

213. What was the name of a weekly magazine read by many Irish immigrants that championed the cause of Irish freedom and fought against "Greenbackism" whose editor, Patrick Ford, also used the magazine as a forum to promote social, political and economic justice?

214. "Tommy the Cork" is a nickname for which well-known friend of FDR?

215. How many American Congressional Medals of Honor were given to Irish-born soldiers?

216. Who was Joseph McGarrity?

217. Who founded the Irish-American Cultural Institute?

218. He wrote a book about American Irish citing their achievements in education and money-making. Who is he?

219. He helped establish the American League and was owner and president of the Chicago White Sox until his death in 1931. Who was he?

220. Who is the Irish Ambassador to the United States?

221. Who was the chaplain for the 69th Regiment—"The Fighting Irish" —during WWI? A statue in his honor graces Times Square.

222. A plumber like his father before him, this grandson of Irish immigrants, brought up in the Bronx and a high school dropout, became one of the greatest labor leaders. Who is he?

223. Who was the Bronx campaign manager who took over James Farley's position in FDR's re-election campaign?

224. His father was part of the 1866 Fenian invasion of Canada; he helped negotiate a settlement in the 1937 auto workers' strike and was appointed associate justice of the Supreme Court by FDR. Who was this red-headed former governor of Michigan?

225. Ronald Reagan comes from the O'Riagain clan and can trace his roots back to what county?

226. What were the "Draft Riots"?

227. What gift did President Kennedy present to the parliament of the Republic of Ireland?

228. A century of Irish political activity, spawned in bitterness and disappointment, culminated in the election of what Irishmen?

229. "Point of order, Mr. Chairman ... point of order." With these words, a senator from Wisconsin who had tyrannized his colleagues and many other Americans was brought down by another Irishman, Joseph Welch of Boston. Who was he?

230. "It is an advantage to be Republican with a Democratic name."—this was spoken by what Democrat-turned-Republican?

231. William Z. Foster and Elizabeth Gurley Flynn, two members of a small band of Irish American revolutionaries, responded to what political ideology?

232. "I am the law," was spoken by what famous political boss?

233. Who founded the political machine that help to elect Richard Daley?

234. Who were the "Know Nothings"?

235. Who was the "Stonewall Jackson of the West"?

236. What brigade did Thomas Meagher, nicknamed "Meagher of the Sword," lead during the Civil War?

237. What was Mary MacGuire's role in the Indian War?

238. John MacDonald and John O'Rourke, architects of the underground, built what famous subway system?

239. "I want you to see about getting a coffin for me. Adieu, boys... all of you must go to my wake at John Daly's cabin tonight." These words were spoken by Bill Buckley at what event?

240. Which chapter of the Land League formed by Judge Thomas Ryan was one of the most active in the West?

241. "The Irish Capital of the West" was a new Ireland built to attract the Irish living in East Coast shanty towns out West. What is the town?

242. What are the "green flags"?

243. Which archbishop warned that the Irish would revenge the burning of one single church by setting fire to the whole city?

244. What organization resorted to violence in frustration over their inability to obtain (by strikes and negotiations) tolerable working conditions and a fair wage for coal miners in Pennsylvania?

245. Who was the First Irish Catholic to ever run for President?

246. Who was the Irishman who arrived in New York, moved to California, struck it rich, and returned to New York a multimillionaire to conquer "polite society"?

247. What was the "right wing" of the Army of Ireland"?

248. His obituary in the London *Times* read, "A most bitter and persistent, as well as most dangerous enemy of this country." Which American Fenian were they referring to?

249. Who was the "Fenian Physician" who made his fortune in America before returning to his native Ireland to help underwrite Irish causes?

250. Who was president of the Ancient Order of Hibernians in 1984?

251. What predominantly Irish Catholic workmen's association, led by Terence Powderly, spawned the American Federation of Labor?

252. Who founded the "last great mining town"?

253. Where does the term "paddy wagon" come from?

254. Where was Cork Row in New York City?

255. Who were the most important men in the Irish communities of the 1800's?

256. Who were the two "honorary Irishmen" from Notre Dame who revolutionized football?

257. Who owns the site where the battle of the Boyne took place?

258. What are the five states with the most residents of Irish ancestry?

259. Who is the executive director of San

Francisco's Irish Forum?

260.	What is the goal of the San Francisco Irish Forum?

261.	What institution offers a degree in Celtic languages and literature?

262.	What famous American woman from New York has been an active member of the Ad Hoc Congressional Committee on Irish Affairs?

263.	In what city in Massachusetts is the "Irish Acre"?

264.	What famous brigade is memorialized by a Celtic cross at Gettysburg?

265.	He parlayed his 50^c a day job as mule driver into a half interest in a towboat that ran between New York City and Albany, and then into ownership of the largest tugboat fleet in New York's harbor. Who was he?

266.	Because the Friends of St. Patrick was originally an exclusive club, the Irish Catholics in New York formed their own club. What was its name?

267.	Where was Victor Herbert born?

268.	What was the first Catholic church in New York City?

269.	He wrote *Butterfield 8* and he resented his Irish heritage. Who was he?

270.	What famous writer used Gaelic names for his childern?

271. Maureen O'Sullivan is the mother of which famous movie star?

272. Who was called the father of the Irish language movement in America?

273. Who is chairman of the Ad Hoc Congressional Committee for Irish Affairs?

274. What three themes are indicative of the history of the Irish in America?

275. Where was the Hibernian Free School — open to students of any religion who had a least one Irish parent — built?

276. Where was the original St. Patrick's Cathedral in New York City located?

277. Ambrose Light in New York harbor was named after what Irishman?

278. Where is Gaelic Park — center of sporting events for many Irish-Americans, both immigrant and native-born?

279. Who immortalized the song "An Irish Lullaby"?

280. Boned Diamondback, Terrapin a la Travers with Bobadillia Amontillado, Chicken Forestiere, boiled bacon, Irish potatoes, and kale, Heidsieck Brut, Demitass, H. Upman Belvederres, and brandy—where is this magnificent repast served?

ANSWERS

GENERAL

1. The Pledge of Allegiance

2. It was Ireland's official color at one time.

3. The harp

4. Brian Boru's harp

5. "God and Mary be with you."

6. The mentally retarded

7. Cobh

8. Anytime

9. A basket-like boat covered with a hide or canvas

10. The clocks on St. Anne's church in Cork

11. If refers to the marshes on which the city of Cork is situated.

12. The were all Cork men.

13. Thomas McCurtain

14. Terance MacSwiney

15. Non-disintegrated traces of plant life

16. In the midlands

17. The Tinkers

18. Poteen

19. The Tinkers

20. The priests

21. 100 yards wide and 108 yards long

22. *Book of Durrow* (650 AD)

23. 40 minutes

24. Women's hurling

25. Connemara

26. To teach Irishmen sword fighting when they were not permitted to use swords

27. The Blackthorn stick

28. An Irish cleric from the 12th century who accurately predicted the sequence of Popes to the present day

29. An ancient Gaelic custom where women loudly wail for a dead friend or relative at the wake

30. Guinness

31. "To Hell or Connacht."

32. Conor Cruise O'Brien, Ireland's most widely known intellectual

33. St. Brigid

34. Monsignor James Horan

35. Muckanaghederdauhaulia,   Co. Galway

36. November 1, a time when dead spirits of ancestors returned to be close to the living

37. No language, no nation

38. Proposals for the political future of Ireland, developed by the constitutional nationalist parties

39. Ballyhaunis, Co. Mayo

40. Lord Michael Killanin

41. 28%

42. Lisdoonvarna, Co. Clare

43. Ernest Walton

44. Between 300,000 and 500,000

45. Shugar

46. Claddagh, Co. Galway

47. Father Neill O'Brien

48. Leader of the Ulster Defense Association (UDA)

49. T.E. Lawrence, whose father was from Co. Meath

50. Irish Wolfhound, Irish Setter, Irish Water Spaniel, Irish Terrier, Kerry Blue Terrier, the Soft-Coated Wheaten Terrier, & the Glen Imaal Terrier

51. Murphy

52. William Rowan Hamilton from Trim, Co. Meath

53. The dandelion

54. The Gaeltacht

55. 15

56. John Tracy from Waterford

57. A raw-hide, heel-less shoe worn on the Aran Islands, suitable for climbing over rocks and in and out of curraghs

58. St. Kevin

59. Margaret Anna Cusack (1829-1899), an early feminist and supporter of Home Rule

60. Eamon de Valera in 1926

61. Founder of the Christian Brothers, born in Co. Kilkenny 1762

62. He was hanged for treason in London, 1916.

63. Patrick Cotter O'Brien, who was 8 ft., 3 in. O'Brien died in 1808.

64. Armagh, with a Catholic and Protestant Cathedral

65. The Liberties

66. Sealinks

67. May

68. A room set aside for aging parents. They acquired title to this room — located in their own home — when the oldest son married and brought his bride home to be the new mistress of his parent's home. Obviously, Irish parents were not eager for the oldest son to marry!

69. Alcohol

70. August

71. The Green Sambo awards issued annually by the editors of *The Irishman*

72. 40.7 million

73. Sean Kelly, world class professional cyclist

74. No one knows — not even the publicists for the exhibit, Con Lynch & Jim Commins

75. Connie Mack for the American League; Mugsy McGraw for the National League

76. Marcus Daly

77. Charles Comisky and Cornelius McGillicuddy (Connie Mack)

78. Christy Ring

79. It was the single largest sporting event ever held for women, with over 10,000 participants.

80. Traditionally, the day when servant girls were given time off to visit their mothers

81. Lawrence Sullivan from Cork, the first chairman of the British East India Company and a member of the British Parliament

82. Whiddy Island at Bantry Bay, Co. Cork

83. John M. Synge

84. No

85. Peat

86. Ian Paisley

87. The Foyle River

88. The Banshees

89. A fairy that often appears in the form of a black horse

90. Halloween

91. Tinsmiths or Whitesmiths

92. Irish "mummers" who attended special events where the "wee folks" are likely to put in an appearance

93. Connemara

94. A sport played on the streets of Armagh and Cork. It is played with a cast iron ball — a "bullett." The object is to get the ball over the finish line with the least number of tosses.

95. Dog races

96. Ten

97. Fuel to generate electricity

98. Dublin

99. Offices of the Genealogical Society

100. White, black and red

101. Athlone

102. A value added tax applied to goods bought in Ireland

103. St. Stephen's Day, December 26

104. Dingle Peninsula, Co. Kerry

105. Lebanon

106. The Irish Declaration of Independence, proclaimed on January 21, 1919

107. W. B. Yeats

108. Five pence

109. St. Patrick

110. Green

111. Beatle John Lennon

112. Prime Minister

113. 1937

114. The lower house of the Irish legislature

115. St. Brigid

116. Bainin

117. Friendship

118. Fidelity

119. Reign

120. Ashford Castle

121. Clifden, Co. Galway

122. An Irish story teller

123. Samuel Johnson

124. $0. Athletes play for the love of the sport; profits are put back into the program.

125. W.B. Yeats

126. Croagh Patrick

127. Ogham, used from the 5th to the 10th century

128. Maeve, Queen of Connaught

GEOGRAPHY

1. South

2. 32,595 square miles

3. 3,500 miles

4. 2400 miles

5. 230 miles

6. Carrantuohill — 3,414 feet

7. Lough Neagh — 153 square miles

8. 4,700,000

9. County Galway

10. Twenty-six

11. Antrim, Down, Armagh, Derry, Tyrone and Fermanagh

12. Dun Laoghaire

13. County Wicklow

14. St. Kevin

15. The Glen of Two Lakes

16. County Wexford

17. River Cullenagh

18. County Clare

19. Connaught, Leinster, Munster, and Ulster

20. Grafton Street

21. Easterly

22. St. George's Channel, the Irish Sea, the North Channel and the Atlantic Ocean

23. 27 acres

24. Ballsbridge

25. Dunganstown — County Wexford

26. Saltee Islands

27. County Louth

28. The Curragh — County Kildare

29. Maynooth — County Kildare

30. St. Colmcille — County Meath

31. Cork

32. Drumcliff — County Sligo

33. County Donegal

34. O'Connel Bridge, Dublin — 150 feet

35. Armagh, Dublin, Cashel and Tuam

36. 85%

37. 11 miles

38. 160 miles

39. County Down

40. Killale Bay

41. Aillwee - County Clare
    Mitchelstown - County Cork
    Dunmore - County Kilkenny

42. Tipperary

43. Thirty-two

44. Neale's Great Musicke Hall on Fish-amble Street, Dublin in 1742

45. Waterford

46. San Francisco

47. Located in Quebec, Canada, it was the quarantine station where Irish entering Eastern Canada were checked. Thousands died there after getting off the plague infested, famine-ridden ships.

48. Achill Island, County Mayo

49. Tacumshane, County Wexford

50. Croke Park, Dublin

51. Killorglin, County Kerry

52. Athlone, County Westmeath

53. Knock, County Mayo

54. It is home of Ronald Reagan's great-grandfather.

55. Brooklyn, New York

56. County Mayo

57. Maynooth

58. Inishmore, Inishmaan, Inisheer

59. Bird sanctuaries

60. Armagh, the Catholic and Protestant center of Ireland

61. Galway

62. Zinc

63. Shannon

64. Located in Antrim, the causeway was formed by cooling lava.

65. Antrim, Armagh, Cavan, Derry, Donegal, Down, Fermanagh, Monaghan, Tyrone

66. Innishannon, County Cork

67. Neugrange, County Meath. It dates back to 3000 B.C.

68. Galway

69. St. Brendan the Navigator

70. Around the Rosquill Peninsula, County Donegal

71. Monserrat

72. Callinstown

73. Cork Hill

74. Elgin Road

75. County Donegal

76. Cork

77. Dublin

78. The south side

79. Fitzgerald Castle

80. Bere Peninsula

81. County Tipperary

82. Munster Province

83. Blackwater, Lee and Bandon

84. County Clare

85. Yeats County

86. Cork County

87. Wicklow Mountains

88. 123 miles

89. Fontenoy

90. 700 feet

91. Clifton

92. Maine

93. Sandycove, Dublin

94. Lough Derg, Co. Donegal

95. Drogheda

96. River Blackwater

97. County Meath

98. Killiney Bay, because of its panoramic background of mountains and sweeping bay

99. The eastern side

100. Aran Islands

101. Ashford Castle

102. Little Skellig Island

103. Cobh

104. Near Dublin - It is a place where dreamers take time out and make a wish

105. Cork

HISTORY

1. A movement formed in 1967 to seek equality in employment, housing, and opportunity for Catholics in Northern Ireland

2. April 15, 1941

3. John Redmond

4. Patrick Pearse

5. 432 AD

6. December 14, 1955

7. Spain

8. July 1, 1681

9. Daniel O'Connell in 1828

10. Eoin MacNeill, commander-in-chief of the Volunteers

11. 1963

12. William Brown from Co. Mayo

13. April 18, 1949

14. Randolph Churchill

15. Kevin Barry

16. Edward Carson

17. The Sunburst

18. A secret peasant society that agitated landlords, tax collectors and tithe gatherers during the 18th century

19. Terence MacSwiney

20. Bernadette Devlin

21. Beal na Blath, Cork on August 22, 1922

22. Charles Stewart Parnell

23. It was the seat of the Kings of Munster

24. Sir Robert Peel, Prime Minister of Ireland during the Great Famine

25. The reign of Brian Boru

26. The "Stone of Destiny" upon which the kings of Ireland took their oath of office

27. Michael Davitt

28. A papal bull issued by Pope Adrian IV granting King Henry II territorial rights to Irish land

29. A general strike by the Ulster Workers' Council

30. General Sir John Maxwell

31. The National League

32. A political concept developed in the 1870's that combined revolutionary conspiracy and open agrarian agitation with parliamentary action

33. The British West Indies

34. In 1795 to combat popery and agrarian disturbances

35. Queen Victoria

36. An agreement between Parnell and Gladstone to end the Land War

37. Armagh

38. Theobald Wolfe Tone

39. Francis Sheehy-Skeffington

40. Walter Raleigh

41. John Holland of Liscannor, Co. Clare

42. In 1887-79 by Michael Davitt

43. Edward Carson, a Dubliner opposed to Home Rule

44. St. Columba

45.   Brian Boru

46.   Henry VIII of England

47.   Queen Elizabeth

48.   Patrick Sarsfield

49.   Robert Emmett

50.   1884

51.   *The Nation*

52.   When Captain Charles Boycott, a
      land agent in Mayo, was effectively
      ignored and ostracized by the com-
      munity

53.   Douglas Hyde

54.   James Larkin and James Connolly

55.   700-900 AD

56.   Robert Briscoe

57.   Irish Parliament was abolished and
      Ireland became part of the United
      Kingdom.

58.   Transferred ownership of the land to
      the farmers who worked it

59.   Apartheid laws which banned Gaelic
      and forbade the adoption of Irish
      customs by Anglo settlers

60.   The flight of the earls, the Battle of the
      Boyne, the influence of the French

Revolution on Ireland, and Parnell's fall from power

61. Kieran Nugent

62. Douglas Hyde from Co. Roscommon

63. Patrick Pearse

64. The *Asgard,* owned by Erskine Childers

65. King James II and William of Orange

66. Maude Gonne, Yeats' lost love

67. Sean MacBridge

68. approximately 60,000

69. The National Guard in the thirties

70. They revoked his membership.

71. "Soldiers of Destiny"

72. Eamon De Valera

73. Dark green

74. The Irish Republican Army

75. Michael Collins

76. Arthur Griffith

77. Eamon De Valera

78. Harry Boland and Michael Collins

79. Sinn Fein

80. He and his men occupied Boland's flour mill.

81. Irish Volunteers and the Citizen's Army

82. Six days

83. 77

84. Francis Meagher

85. Arthur Griffith, Sinn Fein

86. Rory O'Connor

87. Lloyd George

88. The Free State forces opened fire on the Four Courts, which were being held by anti-Anglo-Irish treaty forces.

89. Almost 800 years

90. Slave

91. Between 6000 and 5000 B.C.

92. 1920

93. Sinn Fein

94. Charles Parnell

95. Daniel O'Connell

96. The fields of Clontarf

97. Daniel O'Connell

98. Approximately 8,000,000

99. Catholics were barred from attending Trinity College.

100. Jonathan Swift in an essay promoting human rights in Ireland

101. Approximately one million

102. 1169

103. James Connolly

104. Kilmainham Jail

105. Sean O'Casey

106. Twelfth century

107. A teaching aid

108. "Ourselves Alone"

109. The Invincibles

110. To England

111. Potato blight

112. They promoted nonviolence

113. The Maze Prison

114. Neutral

115. 700 years

116. In Rome — his body was buried in Ireland.

117. Co. Kerry

118. 100

119. Anglo-Irish

120. 1348

121. Destruction of Irish Catholicism

122. Connaught

123. Lord Brougham

124. People who converted to Protestantism for the lower price of food

125. 1,000,000

126. 1,000,000

127. Paul Cardinal Cullen

128. Brighton, England

129. Charles Parnell

130. John O'Mahoney, James Stephens and Michael Doherty

131. The bond of peace between the Protestant and Catholic religions

132. The Catholic tradition

133. The Protestant tradition

134. 27

135. The *Aud*

136. Those indifferent or hostile to Irish Ireland

137. Cricket, rugby and soccer

138.   The Irish Republican Army

139.   James II

140.   Irish and French

141.   Christ Church Cathedral, Dublin

142.   In 1800 by the Act of Union

143.   St. Finbar

144.   The Danes

145.   Human exploitation in the pre-industrial era

146.   A prehistoric burial ground

147.   Oliver Cromwell

148.   40%

149.   1932

150.   1937

151.   The first president elected under the new constitution

152.   The Supreme Council of the Irish Republican Brotherhood

153.   They refused to be seated at Parliment.

154.   Dominion

155.   The oath of allegiance that members of the Irish Parliment had to take to the British Crown

156. Secret voting

157. Distilling, brewing and biscuit baking

158. A political party established in 1929 by the IRA to further its Republican goals

159. To preserve the Irish culture

160. They were leaders of the mobilization of Northern Ireland, which started in 1912.

161. Germany

162. John Redmond

163. Those members of the Irish Volunteers who refused to defend Ireland against Germany

164. Members of the Irish Republician Brotherhood

165. An attempted insurrection

166. The woman who lived with Parnell

167. Six miles

168. Robert Emmet

169. 88,000

170. William E. Gladstone

171. Michael Davitt

172. The Royal Kilmainham Hospital in

Dublin, built in 1684

173. Queensbridge, built in 1764

174. Off the coast of Castletownsend, Co. Cork

175. Thomas Davis

176. 1924, at the Paris Olympics

177. Ignatius Rice

178. Eblana

179. Hibernia

180. James Joyce

181. King Richard III

182. The Cabbage Patch Revolution

183. Hugh O'Neill, Earl of Tyrone, defeated the forces of the Crown, led by the Earl of Essex

184. Four bottles of Guinness

185. James Connolly

186. Robert Mugabe, prime minister of Zimbabwe, who was educated by Irish priests

187. The area outside of Dublin that the English were not able to control

188. John Costello, Taoiseach in 1948

189. 1956

190. 1973

191. Constance Gore-Booth

192. Countess Markiewicz

193. All the rights of Protestants, except for the right to vote or sit in Parliament

194. St. Stephen's Green as second in command

195. Fish

196. From $.50 to $1.50 per day

197. Castle Garden — a fort used in the war of 1812

198. Because he refused to take an oath of fidelity to the Protestant faith

199. The Protestant settlers from England and Scotland who were given land in Ireland taken from the Irish

200. Dr. Tom Dooley

201. *The Boke of the Common Praier after the use of the Churche of England,* printed in 1551

202. 1870-1900

203. Mountjoy

204. St. Patrick's College, Co. Carlow, founded in 1793

205. "The national territory consists of the whole island of Ireland, its islands and territorial seas."

206. Its basis was scrapped and broken Viking longboats.

207. The Oakboys, who tried to drive Ulster Catholics from their land in the late 18th century

ARTS & LITERATURE

1. "The Rising of the Moon"

2. Thomas Davis

3. Thomas Moore

4. U-2

5. Horslips, who flourished during the 1970s

6. A "Feast of Music"—traditional music festivals held in Ireland each year

7. Largely sponsored by the clergy, it was used to eradicate country house dances.

8. The Chieftans

9. Tommy Makem

10. Sean O'Riada (1931-71), who was largely responsible for reviving Irish dance music in the 1960s

11. Edward MacDowell (1861-1908)

12. The jig

13. Queen Elizabeth, who wanted to exterminate all aspects of Irish culture in the 17th century

14. Ed Reavy, originally of Co. Cavan, and a resident of Philadelphia since 1912. He is one of the most prolific composers of Irish music.

15. Francis O'Neill's *Music of Ireland*

16. P.W. Joyce

17. Edward Bunting's *General Collection of the Ancient Irish Music* in 1796

18. The Belfast Harp Festival

19. W. B. Yeats

20. The last of the line of Irish nature poet/musicians

21. An Irish jig and an African shuffle combined, first brought to the vaudville stage by Thomas Rice in the 1840s

22. Bodhrans, which are made from goatskins

23. Michael Considine, born in Spancil Hill, Co. Clare about 1850

24. Turlough MacSweeney, born in Gweedore in 1829, and considered by some to be the greatest Irish piper

25. Bagpipes played by Irish musicians that employ bellows strapped to the player's elbow to generate air

26. Christy Moore

27. "Follow Me Up To Carlow"

28. James Morrison, Paddy Killoran, Paddy Sweeney, and Michael Coleman

29. The Irish Musicians Association. *Comhalt,* with branches all over the world, promotes traditional Irish music, dance and the Irish language.

30. Triona NiDhomhnaill

31. Kevin Barry

32. Considered by many to be the greatest *sean nos* Irish singer of this century, Joe was from Connemara, Co. Galway. (He died May 1, 1984 in Seattle, WA.)

33. A tribute to the great piper from Ennis, Co. Clare. Each year hundreds of musicians gather in nearby Miltown Malbay to participate in musicial events.

34. Declan McManus

35. Turlough Carolan (1670-1738)

36. Derry

37. Born in Dublin, Fields was regarded as one of the greatest pianists of the 18th century.

38. Frank Patterson of Clonmel, Co. Tipperary

39. Paddy Maloney

40. Jack Duggan

41. George O'Dowd, whose father is from Thurles, Co. Tipperary

42. Joe & Mike Flanagan were a popular duo who sang, did comedy and played a variety of instruments on the vaudeville circuit in the 1920s.

43. Van Morrison

44. Luke Kelly

45. Padraic Colum

46. The Abbey Theatre

47. William Butler Yeats

48. William Butler Yeats, George Bernard Shaw and Samuel Beckett

49. Daniel Corkery

50. O'Casey's wife, Eileen

51. Brendan Behan

52. Brendan Behan

53. *Borstal Boy*

54. Lady Gregory

55. Patrick Joseph McCall, born in Dublin in 1861

56. James Joyce

57. 17

58. James Joyce

59. University College, Dublin

60. The play, *A Brilliant Career,* is dedicated to "My Own Soul."

61. *Trinity*

62. Sherwood Anderson

63. *I Follow St. Patrick*

64. Nine

65. The Jesuits

66. "Down by the Glenside"

67. William Butler Yeats

68. Patrick Heaney (music) and Peadar Kearney (lyrics)

69. George Russell

70. One

71. *Playboy of the Western World*

72. Oliver St. John Gogarty

73. The Latin text of the fair Gospels with summaries, commentaries and tables of parallel passages

74. 1904, by W.B. Yeats, Lady Gregory, and Edward Martyn

75. William Butler Yeats

76. The architect who designed Powers Court

77. Castletown

78. Alessandro Galilei

79. Leo Rowsome

80. Frederick Crouch

81. Mr. Dooley

82. Ernest R. Ball of Cleveland Ohio

83. Ethna Carbery (1866-1902) from Co. Antrim

84. "The Patriot Game," written by Dominic Behan

85. William Kennedy

86. Patrick MacGill

87. February 2, 1922, Joyce's 40th birthday

88. Brian Friel

89. Thomas Flanagan

90. John Devoy

91. F. Scott Fitzgerald

92. Brian Merriman

93. Liam O'Flaherty's *The Informer*

94. *Waiting for Godot*

95. Leopold Bloom in *Ulysses*

96. James Joyce

97. George Bernard Shaw

98. Rudyard Kipling

99. Oscar Wilde

100. *Ulysses*

101. Bram Stoker, born in Dublin in 1847

102. William Carleton

103. Seamus Heaney

104. Michael O'Donovan

105. George Bernard Shaw

106. Inishmore, Asan Islands

107. Brendan Behan

108. June 16

109. Flann O'Brien & Myles na Gopaleen

110. Mary McCarthy

111. W.B. Yeats

112. *The Informer*

113. Charles J. Kickham

114.   Ned Harrigan and George M. Cohan

115.   Harrigan and Hart

116.   John Boyle O'Reilly

117.   Seamus Heaney

118.   John B. Keane

119.   Brian Coffey, born in Dublin in 1905

120.   Seamus Heaney

121.   Bernadette Devlin

122.   *Proust*

123.   G.K. Chesterton

124.   Francis Stuart

125.   Brian Moore

126.   Jonathan Swift

127.   "... up railway." — Taken from the folk song, "Poor Paddy, He Work on the Railroad"

128.   Ireland's most famous sculptor

129.   Francis Sylvester Mahony

130.   Erskine Childers

131.   Jonathan Swift

132.   Tom McHale

133.   Hugh Leonard

134.   "The Old Orange Flute"

135.   "Cockles and Mussels"

136.   *The Cattle Raid of Cooley*

137.   George Bernard Shaw

IRELAND-TODAY

1. Neal Blaney & Charles Haughey, both eventually acquitted of smuggling arms to the North

2. Jack Lynch, responding to Derry's battle of the Bogside in 1969

3. Charles Haughey, leader of Fianna Fail

4. An organization wich helps relatives of prisoners in N. Ireland

5. Senator Edward Kennedy

6. To establish a 32-county Republic

7. Civil rights marches from Belfast to Derry were attacked by angry mobs of Unionists

8. Dick Spring

9. Co. Derry

10. The Northern Ireland secretary of state who succeeded James Prior in 1984

11. *Magill,* published monthly in Dublin

12. Patrick J. Hillery

13. *Anois,* published by Gail Linn

14. Cork and Offaly

15. John Hume

16. About 4%

17. In northern Ireland, an informer paid by the Government to testify against others

18. The Brazen Head on Bridge Street, licensed since 1666

19. Bobby Sands

20. Stormont, Belfast

21. The Irish state-sponsored association of artists and writers

22. Gay Byrne

23. 1973

24. Lough Derg

25. No

26. Kevin McNamara

27. Irish missionaries

28. Aer Lingus

29. Michael Noonan

30. Peter Barry

31. Clifden, Co. Galway

32. 1904

33. St. Lawrence O'Toole

34. The Irish Tourist Board, founded in 1952

35. Co. Wexford

36. It was blown up in 1966 by Irish nationalists who resented a memorial to a British admiral in downtown Dublin.

37. The Soviet Union

38. Carlide Bridge

39. Frederick Boland

40. "Ireland Forever"

41. Frank Maguire, who died while in office

42. A law that makes it illegal to display the Irish tri-color in Northern Ireland

43. Lord Craigavon, first Prime Minister of Northern Ireland

44. Rubber bullets, used in Northern Ireland since 1970 against Irish nationalists

45. Irish Police Force

46. Pope John Paul II—nearly 2½ million people attended

47. Cork

48. 1968

49. 99 cents

50. *The Tailor and Ansty* by Eric Cross, published in 1942

51. About 10%

52. Six hours

53. Dr. Noel Browne, minister for health

54. *Irish Independent, Irish Press, Irish Times,* and *Cork Examiner*

55. Betty Williams and Mareid Corrigan

IRISH-AMERICAN

1. San Antonio River, Texas

2. Dunganstown, Co. Wexford

3. New Orleans

4. The Brooklyn Bridge

5. John L. O'Sullivan, editor of the *Democratic Review*

6. Peter Maguire

7. Matthew Brady's photographic gallery

8. Mayor of Indianapolis in 1895, Taggart was from Co. Monaghan.

9. Among Pennsylvania coal miners

10. Mayor Richard Daly of Chicago

11. Tony O'Reilly from Dublin

12. Carlow, Co. Kildare, where the Sisters of Mercy originated

13. The *Brig St. John,* caught in a storm just before landing

14. James Phelan (1897-1901)

15. Massachusetts, with 40%

16. Gulf Oil

17. 35%

18. James Connolly of South Boston, who won the triple jump with a 45 foot effort

19. John McEnroe and Jimmy Connors

20. New York Assemblyman John Dearie's proposal for America to appoint a special envoy to Northern Ireland

21. *Darby O'Gill & The Little People*

22. Filmed in Galway, it starred John Wayne, Maureen O'Hara & Barry Fitzgerald.

23. California with 3.7 million

24. Cornelius Shea of Cambridge, MA

25. Boston College

26. General Thomas F. Meagher

27. John Ford

28. Robert Redford

29. The Ireland Fund

30. The Ozark Mountains in Missouri

31. James Delaney

32. Carmel Quinn

33. Michael Flannery

34. William Kennedy

35. Bishop John Hughes

36. Mary Mallon, the first typhoid carrier recognized in the U.S. in 1906

37. The O'Connells

38. New York City in 1810

39. Woodrow Wilson

40. Father John O'Hanlon

41. John Dunlap from Co. Tyronne

42. His mother, Hannah Simpson, was from Co. Tyronne.

43. 1779

44. Battalions of Irish soldiers who fought for Mexico in the Mexico-American war

45. James Michael Curley

46. Oscar Wilde

47. Charles Lindbergh

48. John Boyle O'Reilly

49. Daniel P. Moynihan at the time of John Kennedy's death

50. Los Angeles, with 1.6 million

51. Ted Kennedy, Tip O'Neill, Hugh Carey and Daniel Moynihan

52. Joseph McKenna, appointed attorney general in 1897

53. Mary Elizabeth Lease

54. Former presidential candidate Gary Hart

55. The Buena Vista Bar in San Francisco, by journalist Stanton Delaplane

56. 291,000

57. John Henning

58. Bernardo O'Higgins, whose father came from Sligo

59. The Irish Communist Party

60. The Algonguins

61. Tim Severin

62. Wyoming and Boone Counties, West Virginia

63. Twelve

64. The first Irish-American literary magazine, edited by James Haltigan in New York City, published in the 1870's and 1880's

65. The Emigrant Savings Bank

66. The Caribbean

67. The Five Points on the Lower East Side

68. Mayor James Curley of Boston

69. Buffalo Bill

70. John Z. DeLorean

71. Jesse Jackson

72. Father Sean McManus

73. A New York - based repertory company in the 1920s that performed the works of Synge, Lady Gregory, Yeats, and Pearse

74. Margaret Mitchell

75. Air National, owned by Peter McGarrity of Co. Clare

76. Robert Kane

77. Carrickfergus, Co. Antrim

78. Maurice N. Hennessey

79. A major figure in the American Labor movement between 1890 & 1930, Mother was born Mary Harrison in Co. Cork in 1830.

80. Cork City, where Ford's father had emigrated from during the Famine

81. Paul O'Dwyer

82. Victor Herbert

83. A collision between a funeral procession and a volunteer fire department truck

84. Father Theobald Matthew, leader of the temperance movement in America in the 1850s

85. The Know Nothing Party

86. The *Amagiri*—a destroyer

87. Barney McGinniskin

88. James McParlan from Co. Armagh

89. The Erie Canal

90. New Orleans

91. 500

92. John Joseph Hughes

93. Colin Kelly Jr.

94. The Fighting 69th from New York

95. Bob Considine

96. President John F. Kennedy

97. Finley Peter Dunne

98. William Grattan Tyrone Power, born in Co. Waterford in 1914—a musician and actor popular in Ireland, England and America

99. 125

100. A term given to Irish actors who black-faced to portray Africans on the vaudeville circuit

101. They occurred when a troop of English actors tried to perform Hamlet in New York and were interrupted by Irish theater-goers.

102. *Abie's Irish Rose*

103. Diamond Jim Brady

104. David O'Docherty

105. A famous labor organizer in the early part of this century who eventually became chairman of the Communist Party in the U.S.A.

106. Henry McCarty, the most notorious gunman of the Old West, eventually killed by Sheriff Pat Garrett

107. Michael Delaney Dowd

108. Actor Pat O'Brien

109. Originally from Derry, Mulligan was a spy for the Americans during the Revolutionary War who saved George Washington from an assasination plot.

110. A Catholic church on the bank of Lizard Creek in Clare, Iowa.

111. Bernard P. McDonough

112. Pennsylvania

113. Sympathetic to Anglo-Saxon sentiment

114. Cotton Mather

115. New Connaught, New Leinster, New Munster

116. 10%

117. 22

118. "Unpack."

119. Father Cormen A. Walsh, OFM who won six decorations for bravery in the Korean War

120. Irish soldiers and aristocrats who fled to France and fought for the Bourbon kings. They wrote to Benjamin Franklin volunteering to fight in the American Revolution.

121. Saturday night parties to welcome the "Greenhorns"

122. John Carroll of Baltimore

123. Dominick Lynch (New York)

124. A 17th century chief of the Delaware Indians

125. Mrs. Richard Carroll Caton

126. They were the two Irishmen to sign the Declaration of Independence.

127. It is to honor the Irish soldiers' contribution to the routing of the British from Boston. George Washington ordered "Saint Patrick" to be the password on March 17, 1776.

128. John Barry from Co. Wexford

129. Comraderie and inexpensive insurance—and because they were excluded from many others

130. Central Park

131. Thomas Fitzpatrick from Co. Cavan

132. The burning of the Ursuline Convent, Charlestown, MA

133. *The Subterranean*

134. Peter Donahue

135. John "Old Smoke" Morrissey

136. Massachusetts

137. The Fighting 69th

138. Franklin Pierce

139. 38

140. James Cardinal Gibbons and Archbishop John Ireland

141. Patrick Quinn, a mineowner—his rise and fall from prosperity

142. The Comstock Lode (silver)

143. John McCloskey

144. Lee McNelly

145. William Marcy Tweed, a friend of the Irish immigrants

146. Prizefighting and gambling

147. John L. Sullivan

148. He established the modern form of boxing by adopting the Marquis of Queensbury rules.

149. 2¼ hours, 75 rounds

150. John Corbett in a match that lasted 21 rounds

151. He became an actor and lecturer on temperance.

152. Irish immigrants' loyalties to America and Ireland

153. William R. Grace (Queenstown, Ireland), elected in 1880

154. John Downey

155. Alfred E. Smith

156. Alfred E. Smith

157. Charles Stewart Parnell

158. "Nuts!"

159. Alfred E. Smith and James M. Curley

160. The labor movement, the Church, and politics

161. They were leaders of political machines at the turn of the century.

162. "The Unsinkable Mollie Brown"

163. 54

164. A disciplinary measure to control underworld warfare. Gangsters who "stepped out of line" would be arrested by Tammany police for carrying a concealed weapon or one that was planted on them.

165. To form political coalitions and to unionize

166. Finley Peter Dunne

167. 14 years

168. Wholesale grocers

169. It helped solidify urban minority support of the Democratic Party

170. Alfred E. Smith

171. William R. Hearst

172. Prosperity and his stand on prohibition

173. William Cardinal O'Connell of Boston

174. James M. Curley

175. Mayor James M. Curley

176. Mayor James M. Curley

177. John P. "Honey" Fitzgerald

178. "Honey" Fitzgerald

179. Puerto Rico

180. John B. O'Reilly, a poet, and Finley P. Dunne, an essayist, jounalist and cartoonist

181. David I. Walsh (1914-1915)

182. James M. Curley (Nov. 12, 1958)

183. John Kennedy in 1963, Richard Nixon in 1971 and Ronald Reagan in 1984

184. F. Scott Fitzgerald

185. Alfred E. Smith

186. Mucker

187. John O'Hara

188. Chicago's Lower East Side

189. "Honest John" Kelly

190. The *Studs Lonigan Trilogy* and the *Danny O'Neill Tetralogy*

191. Philadelphia

192. Eugene O'Neill

193. George M. Cohan

194. George M. Cohan

195. The rise of the prosperous lace-curtain Irish, the faults and failings of the Irish, and the sea

196. Matthew Brady

197. James Hoban from Co. Kilkenny

198. Kathryn D. Sullivan

199. The Indians of the Great Plains

200. Robert Frost at Kennedy's Inauguration

201. Rev. Charles Coughlin

202. Laurette Taylor and Frank Harvey

203. Hugh O'Brien of Co. Fermanagh

204. Ancient Order of Hibernians

205. Arthur Duggan

206. Frank Murphy—mayor, governor, U.S. attorney general, Supreme Court justice

207. Joseph P. Kennedy

208. Franklin D. Roosevelt

209. James A. Farley

210. Patrick J. Hurley and William "Wild Bill" Donovan

211. Woodrow Wilson

212. Fr. John Ryan

213. *The Irish World*

214. Thomas G. Corcoran—Roosevelt's speechwriter, lobbyist, and press secretary

215. 257

216. McGarrity was a key figure in raising money in America for Ireland. Based in Philadelphia, McGarrity was also head of the secret Clan-na-Gael.

217. Eoin McKiernan

218. Andrew M. Greeley

219. Charles Comiskey

220. Tadhy O'Sullivan

221. Father Duffy

222. George Meaney

223. Edward J. Flynn

224. Frank Murphy

225. Co. Tipperary

226. The response of impoverished Irish immigrants to the published list of drafters in the 1863 military draft lottery. Anyone with $300 could buy himself out. Few Irish could apply.

227. The green flag of the Irish brigade which fought in the Civil War

228. John F. Kennedy

229. Senator Joseph McCarthy

230. Senator Joseph McCarthy

231. Communism

232. Frank Hague, Jersey City, NJ

233. Anton Cermak — a Czechoslovakian

234. A political party of the early 1800's bound together by anti-Irish, anti-Catholic sentiment

235. Patrick Ronayne Cleburne

236. The Irish Brigade

237. Her death at the hands of a group of war-painted Indians sparked the Irish sheriff of Bodie and the cavalry under Moses McGlaughlin to hunt down the Indians and turn the tide against them.

238. New York's — tarnished, creaky, but still the arteries of the workingman's commute

239. His hanging — along with McDowell and Daly, who had just shot his 13th victim

240. The Bodie Chapter

241. O'Neill City, Nebraska

242. Regiments from Massachusetts, New York and Pennsylvania which formed the "Irish Brigade" responding to Lincoln's call for soldiers to fight in the Civil War

243. Archbishop John Hughes (NY)

244. The Molly Maguires

245. Charles O'Conner — he ran against Ulysses Grant in 1872

246. John Mackay

247. The American Fenians who in 1867 launched an attack against Canada for the cause of Irish independence

248. John Devoy

249. Pat MacCartan

250. Joseph A. Roche

251. The Knights of Labor

252. John Bodey, an Irish prospector, who had been working his way north of Mono Lake in the Sierras

253. In the 1800's the police wagon would be sent into Irish ghettoes to remove brawling "boyos" — seemed to those "outside" that all Irishmen were named "Paddy," hence the term.

254. The Lower East Side

255. The priests and saloonkeepers

256. Jus Dorais and Knute Rockne

257. James J. Delaney of San Antonio, Texas

258. California, New York, Pennsylvania, Texas, and Ohio

259. James Patrick Goggins

260. A peaceful resolution of the Northern Ireland problem

261. Harvard University

262. Geraldine Ferraro

263. Lowell

264. The Irish Brigade

265. Michael Moran

266. The Ancient Order of Hibernians

267. Dublin

268. St. Peters

269. John O'Hara

270. Eugene O'Neill

271. Mia Farrow

272. Michael J. Logan, born in Co. Galway in 1836

273. Mario Biaggi

274. Poetry, power and liberalism

275. Baltimore, MD

276. Mott Street in Greenwich Village

277. John Wolfe Ambrose, an Irishman, who led the dredging operations in the New York Harbor

278. The Bronx

279. Bing Crosby

280. In New York City at the Annual Society of the Friendly Sons of St. Patrick Dinner — a traditional menu that dates back to Victor Herbert's presidency.